50 Delicious Meals for Two Recipes

By: Kelly Johnson

Table of Contents

- Spaghetti Carbonara
- Chicken Alfredo
- Lemon Herb Grilled Salmon
- Beef Tenderloin with Garlic Butter
- Shrimp Scampi
- Chicken Parmesan
- Caprese Salad with Balsamic Glaze
- Steak Frites
- Teriyaki Glazed Chicken Thighs
- Mushroom Risotto
- Pan-Seared Duck Breast
- Mediterranean Chicken Skewers
- Bacon-Wrapped Pork Tenderloin
- Garlic Butter Shrimp and Asparagus
- Grilled Chicken Caesar Salad
- Pan-Seared Scallops with Lemon Butter
- Eggplant Parmesan
- Lamb Chops with Rosemary and Garlic
- Stuffed Bell Peppers
- Beef Wellington
- Grilled Tuna Steaks
- Roasted Vegetable and Quinoa Bowl
- Chicken Piccata
- Filet Mignon with Red Wine Sauce
- Roasted Salmon with Dill and Mustard
- Shrimp and Grits
- Sweet and Sour Chicken
- Lemon Garlic Pork Chops
- Baked Ziti with Ricotta
- Chicken and Spinach Stuffed Shells
- Grilled Cheese with Tomato Soup
- Eggplant and Zucchini Gratin
- Chicken and Vegetable Stir-Fry
- Chili Lime Steak Tacos
- Pesto Pasta with Grilled Chicken

- Beef and Broccoli Stir-Fry
- Fettuccine Alfredo with Shrimp
- Seared Ahi Tuna with Soy Ginger Sauce
- Teriyaki Chicken and Rice
- Grilled Shrimp Tacos
- Roasted Chicken Thighs with Potatoes
- Veggie-Stuffed Mushrooms
- Balsamic Glazed Chicken with Vegetables
- Garlic Parmesan Steak Bites
- Spicy Thai Basil Chicken
- Beef and Spinach Stuffed Mushrooms
- Seared Scallops with Cauliflower Purée
- Spaghetti with Pesto and Cherry Tomatoes
- Grilled Vegetable and Goat Cheese Salad
- Chicken and Broccoli Alfredo

Spaghetti Carbonara

Ingredients:

- **12 oz spaghetti**
- **2 tablespoons olive oil**
- **4 oz pancetta or bacon**, chopped
- **3 large eggs**
- **1 cup grated Parmesan cheese**
- **1/2 cup heavy cream**
- **2 garlic cloves**, minced
- **Salt and pepper**, to taste
- **Fresh parsley**, chopped for garnish

Instructions:

1. Cook the spaghetti according to package instructions. Drain, reserving 1 cup of pasta water.
2. In a large skillet, heat olive oil over medium heat. Add pancetta or bacon and cook until crispy, about 5-7 minutes.
3. In a bowl, whisk together eggs, Parmesan cheese, heavy cream, salt, and pepper.
4. Add minced garlic to the skillet with pancetta and cook for 1 minute until fragrant.
5. Add the cooked spaghetti to the skillet, tossing to coat. Remove from heat and quickly stir in the egg mixture, adding reserved pasta water a little at a time to reach the desired creaminess.
6. Garnish with fresh parsley and additional Parmesan before serving.

Chicken Alfredo

Ingredients:

- 2 tablespoons olive oil
- 4 boneless, skinless chicken breasts
- **Salt and pepper,** to taste
- **3 garlic cloves**, minced
- 1 cup heavy cream
- 1 cup grated Parmesan cheese
- 1/2 cup chicken broth
- 1 tablespoon butter
- 12 oz fettuccine pasta
- **Chopped parsley,** for garnish

Instructions:

1. Cook the fettuccine pasta according to package instructions. Drain and set aside.
2. Season chicken breasts with salt and pepper. Heat olive oil in a skillet over medium-high heat. Cook chicken for 6-7 minutes per side, until fully cooked. Remove and slice thinly.
3. In the same skillet, melt butter and add minced garlic. Cook for 1-2 minutes until fragrant.
4. Add heavy cream, Parmesan cheese, and chicken broth. Bring to a simmer and cook for 5-7 minutes, until the sauce thickens.
5. Toss the cooked pasta and sliced chicken into the sauce. Stir to combine.
6. Garnish with chopped parsley and serve hot.

Lemon Herb Grilled Salmon

Ingredients:

- 4 salmon fillets
- 2 tablespoons olive oil
- **2 garlic cloves**, minced
- **1 tablespoon lemon zest**
- **Juice of 1 lemon**
- **1 teaspoon dried thyme**
- **Salt and pepper**, to taste

Instructions:

1. Preheat grill to medium-high heat.
2. In a small bowl, whisk together olive oil, garlic, lemon zest, lemon juice, thyme, salt, and pepper.
3. Brush the salmon fillets with the marinade and let sit for 10-15 minutes.
4. Grill the salmon for 4-5 minutes per side, or until cooked through and easily flakes with a fork.
5. Serve with additional lemon wedges, if desired.

Beef Tenderloin with Garlic Butter

Ingredients:

- **2 beef tenderloin steaks** (about 6 oz each)
- **2 tablespoons olive oil**
- **Salt and pepper**, to taste
- **3 tablespoons butter**
- **3 garlic cloves**, minced
- **1 teaspoon fresh rosemary**, chopped (optional)

Instructions:

1. Preheat the oven to 400°F (200°C).
2. Season the beef tenderloin steaks with salt and pepper.
3. Heat olive oil in an oven-safe skillet over medium-high heat. Sear the steaks for 3-4 minutes per side until browned.
4. Add butter, garlic, and rosemary (if using) to the pan. Baste the steaks with the melted butter and garlic.
5. Transfer the skillet to the oven and roast for 6-8 minutes for medium-rare (adjust time for desired doneness).
6. Remove from the oven, let rest for 5 minutes, and serve.

Shrimp Scampi

Ingredients:

- **1 lb large shrimp**, peeled and deveined
- **12 oz linguine pasta**
- **3 tablespoons butter**
- **3 tablespoons olive oil**
- **4 garlic cloves**, minced
- **1/4 cup white wine**
- **Juice of 1 lemon**
- **Salt and pepper**, to taste
- **Chopped parsley**, for garnish

Instructions:

1. Cook the linguine according to package instructions. Drain and set aside.
2. In a large skillet, heat butter and olive oil over medium heat. Add minced garlic and cook for 1-2 minutes until fragrant.
3. Add the shrimp and cook for 2-3 minutes per side, until pink and opaque.
4. Pour in white wine and lemon juice, stirring to combine. Let the sauce simmer for 2-3 minutes.
5. Toss the cooked linguine into the skillet, coating it in the sauce.
6. Season with salt and pepper, garnish with parsley, and serve.

Chicken Parmesan

Ingredients:

- 4 boneless, skinless chicken breasts
- 1 cup breadcrumbs
- 1/2 cup grated Parmesan cheese
- 1 teaspoon dried oregano
- **2 eggs**, beaten
- 2 cups marinara sauce
- 2 cups shredded mozzarella cheese
- **Olive oil**, for frying
- **Fresh basil**, for garnish

Instructions:

1. Preheat the oven to 375°F (190°C).
2. Mix breadcrumbs, Parmesan cheese, and oregano in a shallow bowl. Dip chicken breasts in beaten eggs, then coat with the breadcrumb mixture.
3. Heat olive oil in a skillet over medium heat. Fry the chicken breasts for 3-4 minutes per side, until golden brown.
4. Transfer the chicken to a baking dish. Top each piece with marinara sauce and shredded mozzarella.
5. Bake for 20-25 minutes, until the cheese is melted and bubbly.
6. Garnish with fresh basil and serve.

Caprese Salad with Balsamic Glaze

Ingredients:

- **4 large tomatoes**, sliced
- **1 lb fresh mozzarella cheese**, sliced
- **1/4 cup fresh basil leaves**
- **2 tablespoons olive oil**
- **1/4 cup balsamic vinegar**
- **Salt and pepper**, to taste

Instructions:

1. Arrange tomato and mozzarella slices alternately on a platter.
2. Scatter fresh basil leaves over the top.
3. In a small saucepan, heat balsamic vinegar over medium heat. Simmer for 5-7 minutes until reduced by half.
4. Drizzle olive oil and balsamic glaze over the salad.
5. Season with salt and pepper, and serve.

Steak Frites

Ingredients:

- **2 ribeye steaks** (or your preferred cut)
- **2 tablespoons olive oil**
- **Salt and pepper**, to taste
- **1 lb frozen French fries** or homemade fries
- **1 tablespoon butter**
- **2 garlic cloves**, minced
- **Fresh parsley**, chopped for garnish

Instructions:

1. Preheat the oven to 425°F (220°C). Bake the French fries according to package instructions until crispy.
2. Season the steaks with salt and pepper. Heat olive oil in a skillet over medium-high heat. Cook the steaks for 3-4 minutes per side for medium-rare, or to your desired doneness.
3. Remove the steaks and let rest for 5 minutes.
4. In the same skillet, melt butter and sauté garlic for 1-2 minutes.
5. Serve the steaks with French fries, garnished with parsley and the garlic butter sauce.

Teriyaki Glazed Chicken Thighs

Ingredients:

- 4 bone-in, skinless chicken thighs
- 1/4 cup soy sauce
- 2 tablespoons honey
- 1 tablespoon rice vinegar
- 2 tablespoons sesame oil
- **2 garlic cloves**, minced
- **1 tablespoon ginger**, grated
- **Sesame seeds**, for garnish

Instructions:

1. Preheat the oven to 400°F (200°C).
2. In a bowl, whisk together soy sauce, honey, rice vinegar, sesame oil, garlic, and ginger.
3. Place the chicken thighs in a baking dish and pour the marinade over them. Let marinate for at least 30 minutes.
4. Bake the chicken for 35-40 minutes, basting halfway through with the marinade.
5. Garnish with sesame seeds and serve.

Mushroom Risotto

Ingredients:

- 1 tablespoon olive oil
- **1/2 cup onion**, finely chopped
- **2 garlic cloves**, minced
- **2 cups Arborio rice**
- **1 cup white wine**
- **4 cups chicken or vegetable broth**, warmed
- **1 cup heavy cream**
- **1 1/2 cups Parmesan cheese**, grated
- **2 cups mushrooms**, sliced (such as cremini or button)
- **Salt and pepper**, to taste
- **Fresh parsley**, chopped for garnish

Instructions:

1. Heat olive oil in a large pan over medium heat. Add onions and garlic, cooking until softened, about 3-4 minutes.
2. Add the mushrooms and cook until they release their juices, about 5 minutes.
3. Stir in the Arborio rice and cook for 1-2 minutes until lightly toasted.
4. Add white wine and stir until absorbed.
5. Gradually add the warm broth, 1/2 cup at a time, stirring frequently and allowing the liquid to absorb before adding more. Continue until the rice is creamy and tender, about 20-25 minutes.
6. Stir in the heavy cream and Parmesan cheese. Season with salt and pepper to taste.
7. Garnish with fresh parsley and serve.

Pan-Seared Duck Breast

Ingredients:

- 2 duck breasts
- **Salt and pepper**, to taste
- 1 tablespoon olive oil
- 1 tablespoon butter
- **1 garlic clove**, smashed
- **1 sprig rosemary** (optional)

Instructions:

1. Preheat the oven to 400°F (200°C).
2. Score the duck skin in a criss-cross pattern, being careful not to cut into the meat. Season both sides with salt and pepper.
3. Heat olive oil in a skillet over medium-high heat. Place the duck breasts skin-side down and sear for 6-8 minutes, until the skin is crispy.
4. Flip the duck breasts and add butter, garlic, and rosemary to the skillet. Sear for another 3-4 minutes.
5. Transfer the skillet to the preheated oven and roast for 5-8 minutes for medium-rare (adjust time for desired doneness).
6. Let the duck rest for 5 minutes before slicing and serving.

Mediterranean Chicken Skewers

Ingredients:

- **4 boneless, skinless chicken breasts**, cut into cubes
- **1/4 cup olive oil**
- **2 tablespoons lemon juice**
- **2 teaspoons dried oregano**
- **2 garlic cloves**, minced
- **Salt and pepper**, to taste
- **1/2 red onion**, cut into chunks
- **1/2 bell pepper**, cut into chunks
- **Wooden skewers**, soaked in water for 30 minutes

Instructions:

1. In a bowl, combine olive oil, lemon juice, oregano, garlic, salt, and pepper. Add the chicken cubes and marinate for at least 30 minutes.
2. Preheat the grill to medium-high heat.
3. Thread the chicken, red onion, and bell pepper onto the skewers, alternating between chicken and vegetables.
4. Grill the skewers for 5-7 minutes per side, until the chicken is cooked through and has grill marks.
5. Serve with a side of tzatziki sauce or a fresh salad.

Bacon-Wrapped Pork Tenderloin

Ingredients:

- **1 pork tenderloin** (about 1 lb)
- **8-10 slices of bacon**
- **1 tablespoon olive oil**
- **Salt and pepper**, to taste
- **2 garlic cloves**, minced
- **1 tablespoon fresh thyme** (optional)

Instructions:

1. Preheat the oven to 375°F (190°C).
2. Season the pork tenderloin with salt, pepper, and minced garlic.
3. Wrap the tenderloin with bacon slices, securing with toothpicks or kitchen twine.
4. Heat olive oil in a skillet over medium-high heat. Sear the bacon-wrapped pork on all sides until browned, about 5 minutes.
5. Transfer the skillet to the oven and roast for 25-30 minutes, or until the pork reaches an internal temperature of 145°F (63°C).
6. Let the pork rest for 5-10 minutes before slicing and serving.

Garlic Butter Shrimp and Asparagus

Ingredients:

- **1 lb large shrimp**, peeled and deveined
- **1 bunch asparagus**, trimmed and cut into 2-inch pieces
- **2 tablespoons olive oil**
- **4 tablespoons butter**
- **4 garlic cloves**, minced
- **1 tablespoon lemon juice**
- **Salt and pepper**, to taste
- **Fresh parsley**, chopped for garnish

Instructions:

1. Heat olive oil in a large skillet over medium-high heat. Add the asparagus and cook for 3-4 minutes, until tender-crisp. Remove from the skillet and set aside.
2. In the same skillet, melt butter over medium heat. Add garlic and cook for 1 minute until fragrant.
3. Add the shrimp and cook for 2-3 minutes per side, until pink and opaque.
4. Stir in the lemon juice, cooked asparagus, and season with salt and pepper.
5. Garnish with fresh parsley and serve.

Grilled Chicken Caesar Salad

Ingredients:

- **2 boneless, skinless chicken breasts**
- **Salt and pepper,** to taste
- **1 tablespoon olive oil**
- **4 cups Romaine lettuce**, chopped
- **1/4 cup Caesar dressing**
- **1/4 cup grated Parmesan cheese**
- **Croutons**, for garnish

Instructions:

1. Preheat the grill to medium-high heat. Season the chicken breasts with salt, pepper, and olive oil.
2. Grill the chicken for 6-7 minutes per side, until fully cooked and internal temperature reaches 165°F (74°C).
3. Let the chicken rest for a few minutes before slicing.
4. Toss the chopped Romaine lettuce with Caesar dressing and top with sliced chicken.
5. Sprinkle Parmesan cheese and garnish with croutons.

Pan-Seared Scallops with Lemon Butter

Ingredients:

- **12 large scallops**
- **2 tablespoons olive oil**
- **2 tablespoons butter**
- **2 garlic cloves**, minced
- **Juice of 1 lemon**
- **Salt and pepper**, to taste
- **Fresh parsley**, chopped for garnish

Instructions:

1. Pat the scallops dry with paper towels and season with salt and pepper.
2. Heat olive oil in a large skillet over medium-high heat. Add the scallops and sear for 2-3 minutes per side, until golden brown and cooked through.
3. Remove the scallops from the skillet and set aside.
4. In the same skillet, melt butter and add garlic. Cook for 1 minute, then stir in lemon juice.
5. Return the scallops to the skillet and toss in the lemon butter sauce.
6. Garnish with fresh parsley and serve.

Eggplant Parmesan

Ingredients:

- **2 medium eggplants**, sliced into 1/2-inch rounds
- **2 cups breadcrumbs**
- **1/2 cup grated Parmesan cheese**
- **2 teaspoons dried oregano**
- **2 eggs**, beaten
- **2 cups marinara sauce**
- **2 cups shredded mozzarella cheese**
- **Olive oil**, for frying
- **Fresh basil**, for garnish

Instructions:

1. Preheat the oven to 375°F (190°C).
2. Combine breadcrumbs, Parmesan, and oregano in a shallow bowl. Dip eggplant slices into beaten eggs, then coat with the breadcrumb mixture.
3. Heat olive oil in a skillet over medium heat. Fry the eggplant slices in batches for 2-3 minutes per side, until golden brown. Drain on paper towels.
4. In a baking dish, layer the fried eggplant slices with marinara sauce and mozzarella cheese. Repeat until all ingredients are used.
5. Bake for 20-25 minutes, until the cheese is melted and bubbly.
6. Garnish with fresh basil and serve.

Lamb Chops with Rosemary and Garlic

Ingredients:

- **4 lamb chops**
- **2 tablespoons olive oil**
- **3 garlic cloves**, minced
- **1 tablespoon fresh rosemary**, chopped
- **Salt and pepper**, to taste
- **1 tablespoon butter** (optional)

Instructions:

1. Preheat the grill or skillet to medium-high heat.
2. Rub the lamb chops with olive oil, garlic, rosemary, salt, and pepper.
3. Grill or sear the lamb chops for 4-5 minutes per side for medium-rare (adjust for desired doneness).
4. Optionally, melt butter in the skillet and drizzle over the lamb chops while resting.
5. Let the lamb chops rest for 5 minutes before serving.

Stuffed Bell Peppers

Ingredients:

- **4 bell peppers**, tops cut off and seeds removed
- **1 lb ground beef** or turkey
- **1 cup cooked rice**
- **1/2 cup onion**, finely chopped
- **2 garlic cloves**, minced
- **1 can (14.5 oz) diced tomatoes**
- **1 tablespoon tomato paste**
- **1 teaspoon dried oregano**
- **1 teaspoon cumin**
- **Salt and pepper**, to taste
- **1/2 cup shredded cheese** (cheddar or mozzarella)
- **Fresh parsley**, chopped for garnish

Instructions:

1. Preheat oven to 375°F (190°C).
2. In a large skillet, brown the ground meat over medium heat. Add onion and garlic, cooking until softened.
3. Stir in the diced tomatoes, tomato paste, oregano, cumin, salt, and pepper. Cook for 5 minutes.
4. Add the cooked rice and stir to combine. Remove from heat.
5. Stuff the bell peppers with the meat and rice mixture and place in a baking dish.
6. Top with shredded cheese and cover with foil.
7. Bake for 25-30 minutes, then remove the foil and bake for an additional 5-10 minutes until the cheese is bubbly.
8. Garnish with parsley and serve.

Beef Wellington

Ingredients:

- **2 lb beef tenderloin**
- **2 tablespoons olive oil**
- **1/2 cup Dijon mustard**
- **1 lb mushrooms**, finely chopped
- **2 tablespoons butter**
- **2 garlic cloves**, minced
- **1/4 cup shallots**, finely chopped
- **1/2 cup white wine**
- **1 package puff pastry** (enough to wrap the beef)
- **1 egg**, beaten
- **Salt and pepper**, to taste

Instructions:

1. Preheat the oven to 400°F (200°C).
2. Season the beef tenderloin with salt and pepper, then sear in olive oil over medium-high heat until browned on all sides. Brush with Dijon mustard and set aside to cool.
3. In the same pan, melt butter and sauté garlic, shallots, and mushrooms until the mushrooms release their moisture and the mixture becomes dry. Stir in white wine and cook until evaporated. Let the mushroom mixture cool.
4. Roll out the puff pastry on a floured surface. Spread the mushroom mixture evenly in the center of the pastry, then place the beef tenderloin on top.
5. Fold the pastry around the beef, sealing the edges. Brush with the beaten egg.
6. Bake for 30-35 minutes, or until the pastry is golden brown and the beef reaches your desired doneness (typically medium-rare for beef Wellington).
7. Let rest for 10 minutes before slicing and serving.

Grilled Tuna Steaks

Ingredients:

- 4 tuna steaks
- 2 tablespoons olive oil
- 1 tablespoon soy sauce
- 1 teaspoon lemon juice
- **1 garlic clove**, minced
- **1 teaspoon fresh thyme** (optional)
- **Salt and pepper**, to taste

Instructions:

1. Preheat the grill to medium-high heat.
2. In a small bowl, mix together olive oil, soy sauce, lemon juice, garlic, thyme, salt, and pepper.
3. Brush the tuna steaks with the marinade and let sit for 10-15 minutes.
4. Grill the tuna steaks for 2-3 minutes per side for medium-rare, or longer for desired doneness.
5. Serve with a squeeze of lemon or additional marinade.

Roasted Vegetable and Quinoa Bowl

Ingredients:

- **1 cup quinoa**, cooked
- **1 cup broccoli florets**
- **1 cup sweet potato**, cubed
- **1 red bell pepper**, sliced
- **1 tablespoon olive oil**
- **Salt and pepper**, to taste
- **1 tablespoon tahini**
- **1 tablespoon lemon juice**
- **1 tablespoon olive oil** (for dressing)
- **Fresh cilantro**, chopped for garnish

Instructions:

1. Preheat oven to 400°F (200°C).
2. Toss the broccoli, sweet potato, and bell pepper with olive oil, salt, and pepper. Spread them on a baking sheet.
3. Roast for 25-30 minutes, until tender and lightly browned.
4. Meanwhile, cook the quinoa according to package instructions.
5. In a small bowl, whisk together tahini, lemon juice, and olive oil to make a dressing.
6. To assemble, divide the cooked quinoa into bowls. Top with roasted vegetables and drizzle with tahini dressing.
7. Garnish with fresh cilantro and serve.

Chicken Piccata

Ingredients:

- 4 boneless, skinless chicken breasts
- 1/2 cup all-purpose flour
- **Salt and pepper**, to taste
- 3 tablespoons olive oil
- 3/4 cup white wine
- 1/4 cup lemon juice
- 2 tablespoons capers
- 2 tablespoons butter
- **Fresh parsley**, chopped for garnish

Instructions:

1. Flatten the chicken breasts to an even thickness. Dredge in flour seasoned with salt and pepper.
2. Heat olive oil in a large skillet over medium-high heat. Add the chicken and cook for 4-5 minutes per side, until golden brown and cooked through. Remove from the pan and set aside.
3. In the same skillet, add white wine, lemon juice, and capers. Bring to a simmer, scraping up any browned bits from the bottom of the pan.
4. Stir in butter and let the sauce thicken slightly.
5. Return the chicken to the skillet and coat with the sauce. Cook for another 2 minutes.
6. Garnish with fresh parsley and serve.

Filet Mignon with Red Wine Sauce

Ingredients:

- **4 filet mignon steaks**
- **Salt and pepper**, to taste
- **2 tablespoons olive oil**
- **1/2 cup red wine**
- **1/2 cup beef broth**
- **2 tablespoons butter**
- **1 tablespoon fresh thyme** (optional)

Instructions:

1. Season the filet mignon steaks with salt and pepper.
2. Heat olive oil in a skillet over medium-high heat. Sear the steaks for 4-5 minutes per side for medium-rare, or longer for desired doneness. Remove the steaks and set aside to rest.
3. In the same skillet, add red wine and beef broth. Bring to a simmer, scraping up any browned bits.
4. Stir in butter and cook for 2-3 minutes until the sauce thickens slightly.
5. Pour the sauce over the steaks and garnish with fresh thyme. Serve.

Roasted Salmon with Dill and Mustard

Ingredients:

- 4 salmon fillets
- 2 tablespoons Dijon mustard
- 1 tablespoon honey
- 1 tablespoon olive oil
- **1 tablespoon fresh dill**, chopped
- **Salt and pepper**, to taste

Instructions:

1. Preheat the oven to 375°F (190°C).
2. In a small bowl, mix together Dijon mustard, honey, olive oil, dill, salt, and pepper.
3. Place the salmon fillets on a baking sheet lined with parchment paper. Brush with the mustard mixture.
4. Roast for 12-15 minutes, until the salmon is cooked through and flakes easily with a fork.
5. Serve with extra dill or lemon wedges.

Shrimp and Grits

Ingredients:

- **1 lb shrimp**, peeled and deveined
- **1 cup stone-ground grits**
- **4 cups water or chicken broth**
- **2 tablespoons butter**
- **1 tablespoon olive oil**
- **1 garlic clove**, minced
- **1 teaspoon paprika**
- **1/2 teaspoon cayenne pepper**
- **Salt and pepper**, to taste
- **1/4 cup chopped green onions**, for garnish

Instructions:

1. In a large pot, bring water or chicken broth to a boil. Stir in the grits, reduce heat to low, and cook according to package instructions (usually about 20 minutes).
2. While the grits cook, heat butter and olive oil in a skillet over medium heat. Add garlic and cook until fragrant, about 1 minute.
3. Add the shrimp to the skillet, season with paprika, cayenne, salt, and pepper. Cook for 3-4 minutes until shrimp are pink and opaque.
4. Serve the shrimp over a bed of grits and garnish with green onions.

Sweet and Sour Chicken

Ingredients:

- **1 lb boneless, skinless chicken breast**, cut into bite-sized pieces
- **1/2 cup cornstarch**
- **Salt and pepper**, to taste
- **1/4 cup vegetable oil**
- **1 bell pepper**, diced
- **1 onion**, diced
- **1/2 cup pineapple chunks**
- **1/4 cup rice vinegar**
- **1/4 cup ketchup**
- **1/4 cup soy sauce**
- **2 tablespoons sugar**

Instructions:

1. In a bowl, toss the chicken pieces with cornstarch, salt, and pepper.
2. Heat vegetable oil in a large skillet or wok over medium-high heat. Fry the chicken pieces in batches until golden and crispy, about 4-5 minutes per batch. Remove and set aside.
3. In the same skillet, add bell pepper, onion, and pineapple. Cook for 3-4 minutes until tender.
4. In a separate bowl, whisk together rice vinegar, ketchup, soy sauce, and sugar. Pour the sauce over the vegetables and bring to a simmer.
5. Add the chicken back to the skillet and toss to coat with the sauce. Cook for another 2-3 minutes, until heated through.
6. Serve with steamed rice.

Lemon Garlic Pork Chops

Ingredients:

- 4 bone-in pork chops
- 2 tablespoons olive oil
- **3 garlic cloves**, minced
- **1 lemon**, juiced and zested
- **1 tablespoon fresh thyme**, chopped
- **Salt and pepper**, to taste

Instructions:

1. Season the pork chops with salt, pepper, and fresh thyme.
2. Heat olive oil in a large skillet over medium-high heat. Add the pork chops and sear on both sides until golden brown and cooked through, about 4-5 minutes per side, depending on thickness.
3. In the same skillet, add garlic and cook until fragrant, about 30 seconds. Stir in lemon juice and zest, scraping up any browned bits from the pan.
4. Pour the lemon garlic sauce over the pork chops and cook for another minute.
5. Serve immediately, garnished with extra thyme if desired.

Baked Ziti with Ricotta

Ingredients:

- 1 lb ziti pasta
- 2 cups marinara sauce
- 1 1/2 cups ricotta cheese
- 1 cup shredded mozzarella cheese
- 1/2 cup grated Parmesan cheese
- 1/2 teaspoon dried oregano
- 1/2 teaspoon garlic powder
- **Fresh basil**, for garnish

Instructions:

1. Preheat oven to 375°F (190°C).
2. Cook the ziti pasta according to package instructions, drain, and set aside.
3. In a large mixing bowl, combine the cooked pasta with marinara sauce, ricotta, half of the mozzarella, Parmesan, oregano, and garlic powder.
4. Transfer the pasta mixture to a greased baking dish and top with the remaining mozzarella.
5. Bake for 20-25 minutes, until the cheese is melted and bubbly.
6. Garnish with fresh basil and serve.

Chicken and Spinach Stuffed Shells

Ingredients:

- 20 large pasta shells
- **2 cups cooked chicken**, shredded
- **2 cups spinach**, chopped
- **1 1/2 cups ricotta cheese**
- **1 cup mozzarella cheese**, shredded
- **1/4 cup Parmesan cheese**
- **1 egg**
- **2 cups marinara sauce**
- **Salt and pepper**, to taste

Instructions:

1. Preheat oven to 350°F (175°C).
2. Cook the pasta shells according to package instructions, drain, and set aside.
3. In a bowl, mix the chicken, spinach, ricotta, mozzarella, Parmesan, egg, salt, and pepper.
4. Stuff each pasta shell with the chicken mixture and place in a baking dish.
5. Pour marinara sauce over the stuffed shells and top with extra mozzarella cheese.
6. Cover with foil and bake for 20-25 minutes. Remove foil and bake for an additional 5 minutes until the cheese is melted and bubbly.
7. Serve hot, garnished with fresh parsley or basil.

Grilled Cheese with Tomato Soup

Ingredients:

- **4 slices bread**
- **4 tablespoons butter**
- **4 slices cheddar cheese**
- **2 cups tomato soup** (store-bought or homemade)

Instructions:

1. Heat the tomato soup in a saucepan over medium heat until warmed through.
2. Butter each slice of bread on one side. Place the cheese slices between two slices of bread, buttered side out.
3. Grill the sandwich in a skillet over medium heat until golden brown on both sides and the cheese is melted, about 3-4 minutes per side.
4. Serve the grilled cheese sandwiches alongside the tomato soup.

Eggplant and Zucchini Gratin

Ingredients:

- **1 eggplant**, sliced into rounds
- **2 zucchini**, sliced into rounds
- **1 cup breadcrumbs**
- **1/2 cup grated Parmesan cheese**
- **1/2 cup shredded mozzarella cheese**
- **2 tablespoons olive oil**
- **2 garlic cloves**, minced
- **1 tablespoon fresh thyme**, chopped
- **Salt and pepper**, to taste

Instructions:

1. Preheat oven to 375°F (190°C).
2. Layer the eggplant and zucchini slices in a baking dish.
3. In a small bowl, mix breadcrumbs, Parmesan, mozzarella, garlic, thyme, salt, and pepper.
4. Sprinkle the breadcrumb mixture evenly over the vegetables and drizzle with olive oil.
5. Bake for 25-30 minutes, until the vegetables are tender and the topping is golden brown.
6. Serve warm.

Chicken and Vegetable Stir-Fry

Ingredients:

- **2 boneless chicken breasts**, thinly sliced
- **1 cup bell peppers**, sliced
- **1 cup broccoli florets**
- **1/2 cup carrots**, julienned
- **2 tablespoons soy sauce**
- **1 tablespoon honey**
- **2 tablespoons olive oil**
- **1 garlic clove**, minced
- **1 tablespoon fresh ginger**, grated
- **Sesame seeds**, for garnish

Instructions:

1. Heat olive oil in a large skillet or wok over medium-high heat. Add the chicken and cook until browned, about 5-7 minutes.
2. Add garlic and ginger, cooking for 1-2 minutes until fragrant.
3. Stir in the bell peppers, broccoli, and carrots. Cook until the vegetables are tender but still crisp, about 5-7 minutes.
4. In a small bowl, mix soy sauce and honey. Pour the sauce over the chicken and vegetables, stirring to coat evenly.
5. Serve the stir-fry over rice and garnish with sesame seeds.

Chili Lime Steak Tacos

Ingredients:

- 1 lb flank steak
- 2 tablespoons olive oil
- 1 tablespoon chili powder
- 1 tablespoon lime juice
- 1/2 teaspoon cumin
- **Salt and pepper**, to taste
- **Corn tortillas**
- **Fresh cilantro**, chopped for garnish
- **Lime wedges**, for serving

Instructions:

1. Preheat grill to medium-high heat.
2. Rub the flank steak with olive oil, chili powder, lime juice, cumin, salt, and pepper.
3. Grill the steak for 4-5 minutes per side, or until your desired doneness is reached.
4. Let the steak rest for 5 minutes before slicing thinly against the grain.
5. Warm the tortillas and fill with sliced steak. Garnish with fresh cilantro and serve with lime wedges.

Pesto Pasta with Grilled Chicken

Ingredients:

- 2 chicken breasts
- **1 lb pasta** (penne or spaghetti)
- **1/2 cup pesto sauce** (store-bought or homemade)
- **1 tablespoon olive oil**
- **Salt and pepper**, to taste
- **Parmesan cheese**, grated for garnish

Instructions:

1. Preheat grill to medium-high heat. Season the chicken breasts with olive oil, salt, and pepper.
2. Grill the chicken for 5-7 minutes per side, or until fully cooked. Let rest for 5 minutes before slicing.
3. Cook the pasta according to package instructions. Drain and toss with pesto sauce.
4. Serve the pasta with sliced grilled chicken on top and garnish with grated Parmesan.

Beef and Broccoli Stir-Fry

Ingredients:

- **1 lb flank steak**, thinly sliced
- **1 cup broccoli florets**
- **2 tablespoons soy sauce**
- **1 tablespoon oyster sauce**
- **1 tablespoon hoisin sauce**
- **2 tablespoons sesame oil**
- **2 garlic cloves**, minced
- **1 tablespoon fresh ginger**, grated
- **Sesame seeds**, for garnish

Instructions:

1. Heat sesame oil in a skillet or wok over medium-high heat. Add the steak and cook until browned, about 3-4 minutes.
2. Add garlic and ginger, cooking for 1 minute until fragrant.
3. Stir in the broccoli and cook for another 3-4 minutes, until the broccoli is tender but still crisp.
4. Add soy sauce, oyster sauce, and hoisin sauce, stirring to coat the beef and broccoli evenly.
5. Serve with rice and garnish with sesame seeds.

Fettuccine Alfredo with Shrimp

Ingredients:

- 1 lb fettuccine pasta
- 1 lb shrimp, peeled and deveined
- 2 tablespoons olive oil
- 3 cloves garlic, minced
- 1 cup heavy cream
- 1 cup grated Parmesan cheese
- 1 tablespoon butter
- Salt and pepper, to taste
- Fresh parsley, chopped, for garnish

Instructions:

1. Cook the fettuccine according to package instructions. Drain and set aside.
2. In a large skillet, heat olive oil over medium heat. Add the shrimp and cook until pink, about 2-3 minutes per side. Remove from the skillet and set aside.
3. In the same skillet, melt butter and add garlic. Sauté for 1-2 minutes until fragrant.
4. Add the heavy cream, stirring to combine. Bring to a simmer, then add the Parmesan cheese. Stir until the sauce thickens, about 3-5 minutes.
5. Add the cooked fettuccine and shrimp to the skillet. Toss to coat with the sauce. Season with salt and pepper.
6. Serve with chopped parsley and extra Parmesan cheese.

Seared Ahi Tuna with Soy Ginger Sauce

Ingredients:

- 2 ahi tuna steaks
- 2 tablespoons olive oil
- **Salt and pepper**, to taste
- 1/4 cup soy sauce
- 1 tablespoon fresh ginger, grated
- 1 tablespoon honey
- 1 tablespoon rice vinegar
- 1 teaspoon sesame oil

Instructions:

1. Season the tuna steaks with salt and pepper.
2. Heat olive oil in a skillet over medium-high heat. Sear the tuna for 1-2 minutes on each side, or until desired doneness.
3. In a small bowl, whisk together soy sauce, ginger, honey, rice vinegar, and sesame oil.
4. Drizzle the soy ginger sauce over the seared tuna steaks before serving.

Teriyaki Chicken and Rice

Ingredients:

- 4 boneless, skinless chicken breasts
- 1/2 cup teriyaki sauce
- 2 cups cooked rice
- 1 tablespoon olive oil
- **1 tablespoon sesame seeds**, for garnish
- **Green onions**, chopped, for garnish

Instructions:

1. Heat olive oil in a skillet over medium-high heat. Add the chicken breasts and cook for 5-7 minutes on each side, until fully cooked.
2. Add teriyaki sauce to the skillet, stirring to coat the chicken. Cook for an additional 2-3 minutes, allowing the sauce to thicken.
3. Serve the chicken over cooked rice, garnished with sesame seeds and chopped green onions.

Grilled Shrimp Tacos

Ingredients:

- **1 lb shrimp**, peeled and deveined
- **1 tablespoon olive oil**
- **1 teaspoon chili powder**
- **1 teaspoon paprika**
- **1/2 teaspoon garlic powder**
- **Salt and pepper**, to taste
- **8 small corn tortillas**
- **Shredded cabbage**, for garnish
- **Lime wedges**, for serving
- **Sour cream** or **guacamole**, for serving

Instructions:

1. Preheat grill to medium-high heat. In a bowl, toss the shrimp with olive oil, chili powder, paprika, garlic powder, salt, and pepper.
2. Grill the shrimp for 2-3 minutes per side, until pink and cooked through.
3. Warm the tortillas on the grill for 1 minute.
4. Assemble the tacos by placing grilled shrimp on each tortilla and garnishing with shredded cabbage, lime wedges, and a drizzle of sour cream or guacamole.

Roasted Chicken Thighs with Potatoes

Ingredients:

- **4 chicken thighs**, bone-in, skin-on
- **4 large potatoes**, cubed
- **2 tablespoons olive oil**
- **1 teaspoon paprika**
- **1 teaspoon garlic powder**
- **1 teaspoon thyme**
- **Salt and pepper**, to taste

Instructions:

1. Preheat oven to 400°F (200°C).
2. In a large bowl, toss the potatoes with olive oil, paprika, garlic powder, thyme, salt, and pepper.
3. Arrange the potatoes on a baking sheet and nestle the chicken thighs among them. Drizzle the chicken with a little olive oil and season with salt and pepper.
4. Roast for 35-40 minutes, or until the chicken is cooked through and the potatoes are tender.
5. Serve immediately.

Veggie-Stuffed Mushrooms

Ingredients:

- **16 large mushrooms**, stems removed
- **1/2 cup cream cheese**, softened
- **1/4 cup Parmesan cheese**, grated
- **1/4 cup breadcrumbs**
- **1/4 cup spinach**, chopped
- **2 tablespoons olive oil**
- **1 garlic clove**, minced
- **Salt and pepper**, to taste

Instructions:

1. Preheat oven to 375°F (190°C).
2. In a bowl, mix the cream cheese, Parmesan, breadcrumbs, spinach, garlic, salt, and pepper.
3. Stuff the mushroom caps with the cream cheese mixture and place them on a baking sheet.
4. Drizzle the mushrooms with olive oil and bake for 15-20 minutes, until golden and bubbly.
5. Serve warm.

Balsamic Glazed Chicken with Vegetables

Ingredients:

- 4 chicken breasts
- 2 tablespoons olive oil
- 2 tablespoons balsamic vinegar
- 1 tablespoon honey
- **1 zucchini**, sliced
- **1 red bell pepper**, sliced
- **1 cup cherry tomatoes**, halved
- **Salt and pepper**, to taste

Instructions:

1. Heat olive oil in a large skillet over medium-high heat. Season the chicken breasts with salt and pepper, and cook until browned and cooked through, about 5-7 minutes per side.
2. In a small bowl, whisk together balsamic vinegar and honey. Drizzle the mixture over the chicken breasts and cook for an additional 2-3 minutes, allowing the glaze to thicken.
3. In the same skillet, add the zucchini, bell pepper, and cherry tomatoes. Cook for 5 minutes, until the vegetables are tender.
4. Serve the chicken with the vegetables and drizzle with additional balsamic glaze.

Garlic Parmesan Steak Bites

Ingredients:

- **1 lb sirloin steak**, cut into bite-sized cubes
- **2 tablespoons olive oil**
- **3 garlic cloves**, minced
- **1/4 cup grated Parmesan cheese**
- **1 tablespoon fresh parsley**, chopped
- **Salt and pepper**, to taste

Instructions:

1. Heat olive oil in a skillet over medium-high heat. Season the steak cubes with salt and pepper, then sear them in the skillet for 3-4 minutes, until browned on all sides.
2. Add the garlic and cook for 1-2 minutes until fragrant.
3. Sprinkle the steak bites with Parmesan cheese and toss to coat. Cook for another 1-2 minutes, until the cheese melts.
4. Garnish with fresh parsley and serve.

Spicy Thai Basil Chicken

Ingredients:

- **1 lb chicken breasts**, thinly sliced
- **2 tablespoons vegetable oil**
- **3 cloves garlic**, minced
- **2-3 Thai red chilies**, chopped (or to taste)
- **1 onion**, sliced
- **1 bell pepper**, sliced
- **1/4 cup soy sauce**
- **2 tablespoons fish sauce**
- **1 tablespoon sugar**
- **1/2 cup fresh basil leaves**
- **1 tablespoon lime juice**
- **Jasmine rice**, for serving

Instructions:

1. Heat the vegetable oil in a large skillet over medium-high heat. Add the garlic and Thai chilies, and sauté for 1-2 minutes until fragrant.
2. Add the chicken slices to the skillet and cook until browned, about 5-7 minutes.
3. Stir in the onion and bell pepper, and cook for another 3-4 minutes until softened.
4. In a small bowl, mix the soy sauce, fish sauce, and sugar. Pour the mixture over the chicken and vegetables, and stir to coat.
5. Cook for an additional 2-3 minutes, then add the fresh basil and lime juice. Stir well and cook for another minute.
6. Serve the spicy Thai basil chicken over jasmine rice.

Beef and Spinach Stuffed Mushrooms

Ingredients:

- **12 large mushrooms**, stems removed
- **1/2 lb ground beef**
- **1 cup fresh spinach**, chopped
- **1/4 cup breadcrumbs**
- **1/4 cup grated Parmesan cheese**
- **2 cloves garlic**, minced
- **1 tablespoon olive oil**
- **Salt and pepper**, to taste

Instructions:

1. Preheat the oven to 375°F (190°C).
2. Heat olive oil in a skillet over medium heat. Add the ground beef and garlic, and cook until browned, about 6-8 minutes.
3. Stir in the chopped spinach and cook until wilted, about 2 minutes. Remove from heat.
4. Add breadcrumbs, Parmesan cheese, salt, and pepper to the beef mixture. Stir to combine.
5. Stuff each mushroom cap with the beef and spinach mixture and arrange them on a baking sheet.
6. Bake for 20 minutes, or until the mushrooms are tender and the filling is golden.
7. Serve warm.

Seared Scallops with Cauliflower Purée

Ingredients:

- **12 large scallops**, cleaned
- **1 head cauliflower**, chopped
- **2 tablespoons butter**
- **1/2 cup heavy cream**
- **2 tablespoons olive oil**
- **1 tablespoon fresh parsley**, chopped
- **Salt and pepper**, to taste

Instructions:

1. For the cauliflower purée: Steam the cauliflower until tender, about 10-12 minutes. Drain and place in a blender or food processor.
2. Add butter, heavy cream, salt, and pepper to the cauliflower and blend until smooth. Set aside and keep warm.
3. Heat olive oil in a skillet over medium-high heat. Season the scallops with salt and pepper.
4. Sear the scallops for 2-3 minutes on each side, until golden brown and cooked through.
5. To serve, spoon the cauliflower purée onto plates, top with the seared scallops, and garnish with fresh parsley.

Spaghetti with Pesto and Cherry Tomatoes

Ingredients:

- **1 lb spaghetti**
- **1/2 cup pesto sauce** (store-bought or homemade)
- **1 pint cherry tomatoes**, halved
- **2 tablespoons olive oil**
- **1/4 cup grated Parmesan cheese**
- **Fresh basil leaves**, for garnish

Instructions:

1. Cook the spaghetti according to package instructions. Drain, reserving 1/2 cup of pasta water.
2. Heat olive oil in a skillet over medium heat. Add the cherry tomatoes and cook for 2-3 minutes, until softened.
3. Add the pesto sauce and reserved pasta water to the skillet, stirring to combine.
4. Toss the cooked spaghetti in the pesto sauce, ensuring the pasta is well coated.
5. Serve with grated Parmesan cheese and fresh basil leaves on top.

Grilled Vegetable and Goat Cheese Salad

Ingredients:

- **1 zucchini**, sliced
- **1 red bell pepper**, sliced
- **1 yellow bell pepper**, sliced
- **1 red onion**, sliced
- **1/2 cup goat cheese**, crumbled
- **4 cups mixed salad greens**
- **1/4 cup olive oil**
- **2 tablespoons balsamic vinegar**
- **1 tablespoon honey**
- **Salt and pepper**, to taste

Instructions:

1. Preheat the grill to medium-high heat. Brush the sliced vegetables with olive oil and season with salt and pepper.
2. Grill the vegetables for 3-4 minutes per side, until tender and slightly charred. Remove from the grill and set aside.
3. In a small bowl, whisk together olive oil, balsamic vinegar, honey, salt, and pepper for the dressing.
4. In a large bowl, combine the grilled vegetables and salad greens. Drizzle with the dressing and toss gently to combine.
5. Top with crumbled goat cheese and serve immediately.

Chicken and Broccoli Alfredo

Ingredients:

- 4 boneless, skinless chicken breasts
- 2 cups broccoli florets
- 1 lb fettuccine pasta
- 2 tablespoons olive oil
- 3 cloves garlic, minced
- 1 cup heavy cream
- 1 cup grated Parmesan cheese
- 1 tablespoon butter
- **Salt and pepper**, to taste

Instructions:

1. Cook the fettuccine according to package instructions. In the last 3-4 minutes, add the broccoli to the pot to blanch.
2. While the pasta and broccoli cook, heat olive oil in a large skillet over medium-high heat. Season the chicken breasts with salt and pepper, then cook for 6-7 minutes on each side, until fully cooked. Remove from the skillet and set aside.
3. In the same skillet, melt butter and sauté the garlic for 1 minute until fragrant.
4. Add the heavy cream and bring to a simmer. Stir in the Parmesan cheese and cook for 3-4 minutes, until the sauce thickens.
5. Slice the cooked chicken and add it to the skillet, along with the pasta and broccoli. Toss everything together and serve immediately.

www.ingramcontent.com/pod-product-compliance
Lightning Source LLC
LaVergne TN
LVHW061954070526
838199LV00060B/4108